Parts of My Soul

(A Collection of Personal Poetry)

By Amy Brown

Parts of My Soul

By Amy Brown

Published by Amy Brown

Table of Contents

Part One

First comes Love and Longing

Crush

simple gesture
simple walk
sets fire
a blaze in my soul
I see him daily
in my heart
his smile
and face
throbs my heart
when can I see you
again, crush
laugh at the thought
of being with you
palms sweat near you
voice shakes
you cause that too
quiver of fear
stop of the pulse
the very mention

of you

cause these too

Eyes

Timid but yet brave
Heavy heart but light in load
I must try to look in those eyes
Set about in a face so precious
I shall hold in my heart
I must try this once to look into your eyes
The ones of precious silver that pierce my heart with a stolen breath
I must look into your eyes before
I begin to feel unrest
Lover, you sit near me
Teasing my senses in unknown ways
The sounds far off distant to me
Although only a few feet away
I must try to look in your eyes
For now our hearts have reconnected in the same line and vein
For now our minds stay as one
For now the shine of the sun will blush
Your heart as I lay my ear upon it

The running wild moment of calm peace

Running through time's complexities

I must try to look at those loving eyes

But they bun earnestly honestly to my heart
because I want to cry for our love

Is immense in proportion of tremendous odds

With this I shall try to look in your eyes

But I cannot promise anything

For I am a modest lover with shy observations

I cannot stand to look at those loving eyes of
ebony brown

For the love in them shakes me to my soul

For the longing in them makes me whole

Missing You

Sitting, kneeling in the rain writing down words
which will mean something one day.

My love and soul, so near and far away but yet
part of you stays lingers around like my perfume
on a towel.

The rain, Ah!

So sweetly does it chime with bells wrapped
around antique petals.

Deeply embedded crystals running, dotting on the
sill, sitting in pools with the smell of chamomile.

Dear lover, dear love.

Oh so sweetly, do I crave your touch.

The slightest caress of your hand, breath to mingle
with my own, defining moments of time's own.

Glide gentle bird, siren of the sky to the nearest
branch way up high to escape the pebbles of
delicate rain from your feathers.

The sky may be mourning while I yet yearn and
crave the slightest satisfaction of your presence.

Dear swooning heart, are thou satisfied or not?

I believe I feel a sweet grace of your hand.

I believe I feel the sweet embrace of your arms.

Oh! A circle of warmth golden with your eyes.

Do I miss it? Yes, with every raindrop cried.

The moment you departed I felt already the slight sliding touch of Venus' hand.

She wove a tapestry around my heart and slowly, she unwinds it whenever you depart.

Sadly though, surely the day draws on without you.

The nights Oh! The nights!

Do not remind me of the solitude.

For woe's shame upon my breast do I desire to feel your warmth

to feel your fire near my bed.

Lover, I miss your time you spent so carefully with me.

I do crave you, love you, want you.

The same as you do to me.

Your hand in mines, the simplest of gestures stirs my soul and imagination.

You light my dark seeded path and shine the sun near my eyes.

Easy, simple, plainly so, for eternity and forever do I believe is to be both you and me.

Illuminate, enlighten, care to learn as to why my heavy heart does not carry a stones' load anymore?

Care to know what I think of you?

I believe you can mirror your thoughts to mine.

Sweet, sweet polite rain.

Sweet, sweet justice.

Washing away the sinful earth beneath my feet,
watching it drip ever so steadily unto the ground
collecting into a miniature sea.

Rain, rain so pure, so sweet…

Oh! How my longing is reflected in you-we.

God's tears, joys and tribulations all hidden in you
like a secret

Do you see this, lover?

Do you see me writing, admiring from my
window pane?

So serene, so peaceful .

Dear sleep wash over me, with gentle curtains
pulled to close over my eyes

into my mind.

So close the door and sleep till mourn.

Love's presence will have to wait at the door.

For I have found enough words,

while this rain falls.

Eternity and Forever

The march was long but now I can finally say
That all was to just find you one day
To march together in life after dawn
Would be the perfect gift
If you allow me to move on
I must say the friendship was a treasure
I must say I loved the full passion pleasure
But now let us keep one promise to each other
Say that you will love me for eternity and forever
The day does draw on
But I drew from you fro power
Enough to boost me through the day
And forever
But now love as we stand here today
Will you promise me this
A simple request I ask of you
Eternity and forever
God the one who sits up above
Has allowed us this one chance

In a lifetime

I was lucky to see you

And meet you so greatly

But can you promise from your lips an eternity and forever

It's a commitment to make from a lifetime of waiting

Cherishing each other's thoughts and love

But now that we are more that friends

Can you promise me this one last time

Before the final plunge

I wish this was over and done

But before we cross out into the world

Defying all odds

And begin each other's wills

Will you promise me a love to transcend time

Forever an eternity you and I

Will you truly be there and care for

Will you stay through sickness and death

Will you be true

Will you leave if you had to

These things we must think of

For they will happen for an eternity and forever

The march was long

The journey a struggle

But now my love sit by me and treasure

Will you promise me this

Since I have already done the same

On this our wedding day

That you can stay by my absent ways

That you can withstand my anger, the tears and joys

My success my failures and most of all

Any children in the future

Can you stand me and my mess

My papers my files and folders laying array

If you had to stay with one for a lifetime

Can you promise me that I am her

And you can love me for an eternity and forever

When My Heart Speaks

My heart speaks truth
undeniable love it feels
for you
the one I've imagined
in my dreams
of a night sky
filled with stars
so bright!
and...oh!
Those eyes you gaze upon me
so loving...
Peaceful yet mysterious to me
they hold a secret that
has yet revealed itself to me
one I want to know so
badly it aches my heart
you speak unto to me
of wonders I have yet seen
wonders you can show me

wonders of purity and
nothing false
your eyes tell the truth
your words do
your gentle hand
so welcomed
so cherished by me
roams around my body
a warm circle you
embrace me in
as your warm voice
warm and deep
continues to tell me
of wonders I have yet seen
My heart it speaks to you
give me your hand
take me to a place
so far form here
away for the crowds
away form the stress
somewhere warm
where our hearts will

speak forever more
to each other
and like a dream
like all other dreams
you fade from my sight
an angel in the mist
but my heart still speaks
come the one I cherish
come and take me away
from the world
take me away
in your arms

Truth

The very concept had escaped my mind quite a few times

for you see

I never did believe in a love that could be

so that is why I kept my feelings inside

in hopes that hiding my true feelings will not show through

even though I tried, I dare say, to lie

I guess my eyes revealed my secret world to you

I tried desperately to see inside of you

but with no luck or avail

It seems I couldn't get the best of you

for you see

I never did make the first move

Every day I thought you and me

in hopes we could be

but with no luck nor action

I quickly subsided without satisfaction

I know it sounds lame

but I did not want to fan the flames

or get hopes up too high
only to have them then bought out of the sky
So I proceed just to be the friend you need
without the need to feel completed
so I became a friend in need
but now I look
four years it took
the tedious time of knowing you
completed us anew
now we stand as one
my love
no more unrequited lust
no more unrequited love
now we stand complete
for it's you and me
friends become lovers so easily
It's no hard to see
we were more of friends than we intended to be
so love, you ask me now
why the smile upon a face so gentle as mine
I simply ask you to know it's true
to satisfy a desire that burned so heavily for years

all the same
it nearly bought you to tears
I must say I'm sorry for my other travels
but they seem so nice and willing to sacrifice
a little to get a lot out of my heart
but now I'm glad, happy
not sad
that it took so long to perfect our union
it took so long to see each other
in a whole new light
because of our one 'reunion'
now we stand with a new union
one full of love shared so freely
back and forth
so love, I ask you a question
why wait so long to quest then?
I know you think I'm sometimes
gentle and kind
but yet villainous and evil
but it's hard for me to believe
that we knew what our hearts wanted
but yet did not approach it

I do regret taking so long
but as you can see
there is no need for alarm
for I have already vowed
my heart to you
to also stay faithful and true
So I began this poem to you
for it only took me not an hour or two
but just five minutes to conduct this to you
so do you believe my words true
if not then here is why I chose you...
Nice and kind, frighteningly loyal
once in love, though she never trusted
I could see a heart of gold
one that needed someone to hold
thought my dreams I thought it to be me
even if you were holding the ...well other
in you I saw humanity
not a monster, a human just like me
someone who needed to be understood
not told, not threatened to be what you could
but someone who needed time to think

about yourself, life and it's many gates
not pressured, not seeking for a prize
just someone you needed to see though your eyes
I must admit I am glad I am her to you
someone who wants to see it through and through
for you I will suffer through hard unkind times
for you I will be there no matter the time
so do you believe me, my answer true
or do I have more explaining to do

Part Two

All the Things I loathe

Pretty, Pretty Lie

What a pretty, pretty lie!

The words that spill forth from your lips.

Hang on the air on whatever they can find.

What pretty, pretty words!

As they intertwine, in and out the realm of fantasy.

You must be a pretty, pretty good fortuneteller.

No?

Then you must be a pretty, pretty good warn spinner.

No?

Then what a pretty, pretty lie you tell!

For I know it's not the truth.

What pretty, pretty words that you tell!

I heard those very words, but in so many different ways.

I have heard those words before when my heart would break and fall.

Now, I have a pretty, pretty lie with pretty, pretty words to tell you.

I never loved you.

See those pretty, pretty words hang in the air?
On whatever they can find.
So tell me more pretty, pretty lies.
So that I may tell you more pretty, pretty words.

Very Light Love

Do sigh and let out that breath that you have been holding since the day I left.

Do you know of the times that I lay awake at night thinking of the times we have shared?

Thinking of how much I loathe and bear your love like my heart on a sleeve,

Your love which did suffocate me.

I drowned not knowing the consequences of my love that you held so to your own heart.

I drowned in bliss and loneliness while you were away to play.

Oh… how I wished you could have seen the love within my arms and not her arms.

At home was where you were supposed to be not in her own.

You left me and I did cry.

But now those tears have dried.

I will not suffer for your mistake.

I will not cry a tear for your disgrace.

I will move on no matter what.

Keep calling dear, I'll just hang up.

Keep trying honey; I'll leave the door locked.

You gave up but I never did give up on a love with another man,

Waiting to receive as I would give up so gladly.

He will keep the hearth warm and stay true to my love;

Never to regret his love.

I do regret you.

For you are: another bump on the log, another dent in the shoe.

You matter nothing to me now for he treats me better than you could.

I do remind you that nothing's change.

You are still the ever shining disgrace.

I shudder to tell him of you.

I shudder to remember of the times I threw away wasting on you.

No need to bother for I am healed.

No need to tell for I am free.

Ready to believe in Love's newest kiss.

The one I had before missed.

I can say now that without you I would have never learned what men to avoid

Tale of Two Lovers

He gives.

She takes.

He looks.

She blind.

He win.

She loses.

He deaf.

She hear.

He afraid.

She brave.

He fought.

She lost.

He battle.

She won.

He was.

She was not.

He be.

She is.

He struggle.

She relax.

He stayed.

She come.

He gave.

She took.

He lost.

He win.

He loved.

He sworn.

He knew.

He lost.

But…

She won.

She lost.

She loved.

She sworn.

She knew.

She lost..

Sad tale

To be told

Heartache to be won

To be lost

To be forgotten
To be known
To struggle
How could this not?
Be so vain
The tale of two lovers
Who's to blame?

Words that Flow So Easily

the words that flow so easily
between you and me
must mean something
other than harmony
the words that hang in the air
the air between you and me
the scant filled air
the beautifully filled air
the words that hang
between you and me
the words that fall so easily
said with such faith
said with such hate
those words we want to take back
those words we regret

Learn to Move On

I never wanted to hurt you
I just wanted to be the one
I never wanted to maim
I only wanted to be with you
It's funny to look back and see what my heart caused
I didn't know I would hurt you so
I didn't know I would end up heartbroken
Was it the words I said?
Was it the anger within my eyes?
It's hard for me to pinpoint which one it was.
I know it is hard to love someone else besides you.
It should be easy to love another.
So maybe it was for the best.
The best of both you and me
I feel sometimes the heart breaking denial that I have put myself through
Maybe if the shoe was on the other foot
We would be able to know what went wrong

But alas! It is not

And what has happen has transpired without additional know-how

How will you choose to remember me?

Would it be in kind words or harsh?

Would it be with a smile or tear?

I wish there was a rewind to life

But then it wouldn't be life at all.

That is why when we make mistakes and hurt the ones we love

That we apologize and at best of times learn to move on

So maybe that is what I have to do with us

Learn and move on

Dark Coiled Heart

with in the dark
with in my plight
sits the lonely heart
within its shell
beats only once
during its dark prison
coiled on all sides
a heart of stone
impregnable to the human eyes
impossible to see for love
has not knocked at its walls
for a long time
the dark coiled heart
sits alone with in its shell
the days of dark covering it
like a veil
it promises no one
who dares to come
it promises nothing

to those who try
and so the dark
heart will sit alone
for all to know
that its loneliness
is forever more

Part Three

Recovery is a State of Mind

Free to Love

Come one! Come all!

Here, here I have a sale for you, mister!

Free to love! Free to love!

One woman free to love!

She has only been slightly used.

She has only been slight abused.

However, she is still perfectly good and free to love!

I know what you are thinking!

Why are you selling once perfectly good woman?

Why would you be selling this wonderful human being?

Well, I'll tell you why…

I recently acquired this free to love woman one day

After a breakup and slight wear and tear,

You see her past relationships put a deep hole in her heart.

You see her past boyfriends and others abused her love.

Now here she stands waiting for love,

for she is free and willing to find a new start.

Please excuse the baggage she had packed behind her now.

If you buy, she will try to rid it.

Free to love! Free to love!

She only as minor damage!

You see before I found this woman,

She was alone and suffering.

She was hurt and in pain.

I have fixed her up, brand new.

With a new attitude, new heart and a willingness to be open,

She is waiting of another love.

Another man who would see her as a partner and not a burden.

Another love that is willing to accept mistakes and forgive.

Another person who will not throw it away for one night with another.

She is looking for championship and a love.

she is looking for a friend and a man.

Free to love! Free to love!

One perfectly used and abused heart with a woman who is free to love!

Do you want to know, sir, how I know she is free to love?

Because that woman is me.

Plain Jane

The plain Jane I was before had to grow and mature

I never was too girlie, just a little burly

For I was a tomboy with jeans and shirts

I never took the time to mature

But once I did you can guarantee

I began to dress ever so womanly

Maybe it's was the world experience

But I tasted life's gold it didn't make sense

The freedom I crave but security I want

The forever in a day adventure were wanted

I craved the wings you'd given me to fly

But most of all I didn't want to say goodbye

So this woman I've matured to

Does it make you notice me too?

I try so hard to dress in beautiful things

But it's like a cow in stripes

So I guess this isn't for me

A mask, a parade without true meaning

My feet notice the shoes I wear
I have pain in high heeled affairs
Notice my dress or skirt
How I walk with a sway
Maybe I shouldn't try theses feminine things
I'll never get why women dress
So much for success
Give me a good pair of jeans
Matching sweat, I'll be fine
But do you even take the time
To notice that I'm just comfortable
For me, no one else influences
My fashion needs
I like being me
Or do you need
One up to date on clothes
For we all surely know
That I'm too plain
Too tall
Too small
Too quiet
Just maybe too loud

But how could I be
All these things
At once
So let me be
I dress un-girlie
I want to be loose and free
So what with a bra
Too confiding and restricting
So what with a skirt
Too much freedom between the knees
So what with jewelry
Give me a ring
No more necklaces
Weighing me down
So I'm a plain Jane
With appreciation for beauty
So what if I'm not
Too girlie

Free to Love Me

I can walk now without hiding my face
I can smile now without a frown trace
I can look around and find who I want
I can dance around without another thought
I have held back the many years and months
Laying in wait
Now I can truly be who I want to be
I no longer have to wait
Wait on hands and knees waiting for you
To come to me
I can call the many numbers and smiles with faces
I can court whomever I please
It is no longer about you
It is no longer about waiting for that one day
It's no longer about please another needs
All those things I wished from you, I want no more
I want o live for my happiness and me
I want to love someone who wants t love me

You see I finally know how to love me

To never expect perfection

To never expect disappointment

Just to live and breathe by myself, relying on no one else

I have found that waiting on one to love me

Was an unnecessary goal

I love me and all of me

Flaws, imperfections and all

I love me for being me

That one truth is true

Until the day I find

A real man who will love me right

Map to Me

I took a map to help
I had a flashlight ready in my hand
I had the will and determination to follow this through
What I had was the map to Me
And finding my true destiny
What I found instead of directions to Me
Was twist and turns that bump me along the way
The way to Me is covered in them
Within holes and pots cut into the middle
I thought I would find the way to Me
Without any distractions or side trips
However, I found that the path to Me was not clear and set
I roamed the way, searching, looking
Looking and searching to no avail
It is hard to find Me
In the clouds of fog and mist
I am still finding Me,
Wandering through dusk and dawn

Still finding Me while using this map
Unsure if I would find Me before my time is up

Life After

I have wondered for the longest time

How life would be after you

Here I am now

Naked and ashamed, waiting for the whole world to know of me

My heart shattered broken upon the ground

Just waiting, waiting for the final blow

Yet no matter how many times

It braces itself for that awaiting blow

Does it beat again and jump back up

In cheerful glee and half expecting anxiety

I knew that one day this would come

Myself alone and letting you go.

But I never knew that it would be so soon

I never knew it would hurt so hard

Still like the old adage claims

I survive what I thought would undo me at the very ends

I have cried and shed my last few tears of sympathy

I have consoled myself one less lonely night

In the lonely throes and angry woes of a woman scorned

Despite the worries, woes and hurts

I still am able to survive without you

And for you, I am thankful

For both the good and bad memories I must hide within myself

For your see without the good I would not be able to see it in others

For without the bad, I would not know what to look for

I can take confidence in the fact that

Life without you would be something I cannot miss

There will be others or maybe just one

There will be someone who loves me honestly and truly

Maybe I will find him or maybe I won't

Finding him will be the adventure

An investment in a life time of surprises

To think that so many months ago

I believed life without you was not worth much

To think I use to catch my breath at the very thought

But it seems now I have outrun those silly ideas

And found my own footing on the ground

Part Four

Dedication to those who inspire

Looking Alive

Staring up at the ceiling
yet not knowing whether to
I am still breathing
I stare into an abyss where the time
and reality never ceasing to exist
in the treacherous world where the
human mind seems to stop
in questions and thoughts that randomly zoom
by in a flash or in a state
that seems to sedate my frame of mind
I try and try but I can't seem to take the time
to stop and appreciate
the flowers, though ironically, I've got allergies
seem to smell sweet sweet
like rain showers in July and May that litter the
ground
with innocent play
like beautiful snow that plaques the ground
with layers of pure white

playing around in the air
the ceiling does no justice to the playing in my head
the top does not do my brain fair
As expected as can be
I look alive and still dead in the middle of the floor
playing with my hair and looking up above
I can see things that no one else can
I can see heaven in the eyes of a lover
I can see heaven when I look at my grandmother's grave
I can see even when I'm blind
and sometimes I wonder how can one who's
blind see so perfectly the world in another view
it's ironic and it's strange
but then again the world does not hand you apples
when you ask for oranges or grapes
the world is not a pearl or oyster but
something ironic sitting in a galaxy
rotating on its own
around one golden star facing
eastward or westward

either way it goes
the faces stay the same
you would never notice anyone
if they all didn't become a normal blur
that you pass everyday
the ceiling does no justice to my mind play
the ceiling does no justice to my fair play
looking alive and staring up out of the floor
boring my brain with thoughts of amour
I can see myself in years from now
I can see myself in days again
looking at the mirror
does no justice
looking at the mirror
I still see the same world
wishing for the ending
wishing to see the beginning
does the world puzzle you not
with it's confusing puzzles
and light hearted life
staring up out of the floor and pretending to be alive

seems to be the best way to summarize
the world's view

Tall as a Redwood

(Dedicated to Quentin)

It has been a long journey, one filled with beginnings

And, my loved ones, this is just one ending

Of a novel, of a story among many others

Let them say I stood as tall as a redwood

Let them say I was more than a man

Let them say I shared in the joy of life

Let them say my laughter was infectious

I have loved and been loved greatly

Know that I love all of the good times

Let them rouse a sounding cheer

One to drown out the trumpets of heaven

Let them pray and hear the words spoken

Let them speak in tones of reverence about the man I was

Let them know that for years to come I will still be there

-Never to be forgotten-

Let them say what they will of me as long as I
have your love

When I come to those gates, I will give my love
and stories to those who have passed before me

I will tell them of my time and whisper the jokes I
have learned

So I ask, not for you to cry, but rejoice in the time
I was here

Recall the laughs and joys I have shared with you

Recall the times where we were happy

Let them know I'm fishing

Let me depart with your words of love as I have
left you with words of wisdom

I will live on within your heart and memories

Tiny Joy

(Dedicated to babies)

soft black
beautiful light
born into the world
from an unknown place
sweet little face
with eyes of joy
wondering how
she came to be
with curly hair
of black ebony
examining her surroundings
feeling a little different
small yet fragile
breath of life
healthy and
bouncing
up and down
laughter of joy

Role of Women

(To my Heroines)

Some say that a strong headman builds a mighty village.

But the force driving him is a strong woman.

A strong fortress cannot stand without its support.

A brave emperor cannot continue a dynasty without a strong woman.

A child cannot grow without a loving mother.

A life does not begin without a touch of light entering its path.

A life does not end without the dimming of that light.

Some say that a strong headman builds a mighty village.

But it's his wife that drives him.

A clan cannot be without a leader.

A tribe cannot thrive without food.

A religion cannot preach without a preacher.

A headman cannot build a mighty village without his wife to drive him.

A child cannot learn without a teacher to teach him.

A child can kill without someone to care.

A child cannot sleep without a light to drive the monsters away.

A child cannot thrive without someone to show him the way.

A man cannot be without a mother.

A man cannot be whole without a wife to love him.

No matter what anyone says the world cannot be right without a woman driving it on.

###

Thank you for reading!

About the Poet

Full time mother and administrative assistant that is what I am now. I have been writing since I was a kid. I know this because I have an award from second grade. I've been on and off for a few years, occasionally dipping my toe back into the world of writing. I have been writing poetry and fiction for number of years now but never had the courage to publish them. Most of my work is very private with the exception of allowing family and friends to read them. I love books, music, games and my family. Look for more of my books coming soon. Thank you so much for your support!

Connect with me:

Smashwords:http://www.smashwords.com/profile/view/amymbrown

AuthorsDen:
http://www.authorsden.com/amymbrown1

www.ingramcontent.com/pod-product-compliance
Ingram Content Group UK Ltd.
Pitfield, Milton Keynes, MK11 3LW, UK
UKHW020217250726
13967UKWH00001B/50

9 781105 420870